Accelerated Christian Training Series

Laying the FOUNDATION

BOOK 1

THE NATURE OF GOD

Dr. Mark Hanby

© Copyright 2001 — Mark Hanby Ministries

All rights reserved. This book is protected by the copyright laws of the United States of America. This book may not be copied or reprinted for commercial gain or profit. The use of short quotations or occasional page copying for personal or group study is permitted and encouraged. Permission will be granted upon request. Unless otherwise identified, Scripture quotations are from the New King James Version of the Bible. Scripture quotations marked KJV and AMP are taken from the King James Version and the Amplified Bible, respectively. Emphasis within Scripture quotations is the author's own. Please note that Destiny Image's publishing style capitalizes certain pronouns in Scripture that refer to the Father, Son, and Holy Spirit, and may differ from some Bible publishers' styles.

Take note that the name satan and related names are not capitalized. We choose not to acknowledge him, even to the point of violating grammatical rules.

Destiny Image® Publishers, Inc.
P.O. Box 310
Shippensburg, PA 17257-0310

"Speaking to the Purposes of God for This
Generation and for the Generations to Come"

ISBN 0-7684-2142-X

For Worldwide Distribution
Printed in the U.S.A.

This book and all other Destiny Image, Revival Press, MercyPlace, Fresh Bread, Destiny Image Fiction, and Treasure House books are available at Christian bookstores and distributors worldwide.

For a U.S. bookstore nearest you, call **1-800-722-6774**.
For more information on foreign distributors,
call **717-532-3040**.
Or reach us on the Internet: **www.destinyimage.com**

Contents

Introduction 5

I. The Nature of God 9
    A. Who Is God?
    B. How Is It Possible for Man to Know God?
    C. What Is God?
    D. What Qualities Might We Use to Describe God?
    E. What Does the Term *Triune Godhead* Mean?
    F. What Is God's Name?
    G. What Is the Difference Between the Lord of the Old Testament and the Lord of the New Testament?
    H. Who Is the Holy Spirit and How Is He Related to Jesus Christ?

II. The Bible 35
    A. What Is the Bible?
    B. What Are the Results of Obeying the Bible?
    C. What Are the Two Great Divisions in the Bible?
    D. What Are the Books of the Bible?
    E. What Are the Benefits of Studying the Bible?
    F. How Often Should We Read From This Collection of Books?
    G. What Other Books Should Supplement My Study of the Bible?
    H. What Should We Do After Reading the Bible?

III. The Creation 55
    A. What Did God Create?
    B. What Did God Create First?
    C. What Are Angels?
    D. What Does the Bible Tell Us About Good Angels?
    E. What Does the Bible Tell Us About Evil Angels?
    F. Are Angels to Be Worshiped?
    G. Who Is Lucifer?
    H. What Is Hell?
    I. Who Has Power Over Satan and His Demons?
    J. What Did God Create After the Spirit Realm?

Introduction

And you shall know the truth, and the truth shall make you free (John 8:32).

What Is Truth?

Truth Is a Person

"What is truth?" Pilate asked Jesus (Jn. 18:38). The answer to Pilate's timeless question was standing before him. Truth is not a series of facts or the sum of information. Truth is a Person: Jesus Christ. Jesus said of Himself, "I am the way, the truth, and the life" (Jn. 14:6). Truth is not only rational, it is relational. Religious theory that only teaches about God can never liberate the soul. True freedom is found in knowing Him. "And ye shall know the truth, and the truth shall make you free" (Jn. 8:32).

God has chosen to unfold His relational truth in various ways throughout the Bible and always in the form of personal relationship between Himself and men such as Adam, Noah, and Abraham. The unfolding revelation of God's relationship with man was spelled out in agreements between God and man called covenants. What better way to unfold a relational truth than in the context of relationship?

Truth Is the Result of Seeking Jesus

This relational truth is more than experience. Despite his great experience on the road to Damascus, the apostle Paul did not end his search for truth but wrote, "...that I may know *Him* and the power of His resurrection, and the fellowship of His sufferings..." (Phil. 3:10, emphasis mine). Job, wounded and in distress, cried out, "Oh that I knew where I might find *Him*..."

The Nature of God

(Job 23:3). Jesus said, "Blessed are those who hunger and thirst for righteousness, for they shall be filled" (Mt. 5:6). Our finding the truth is the result of a hunger to know the Person of Jesus Christ. We do not seek truth and find Jesus; we seek Jesus and find the truth.

Truth Is a Highway

We may think of truth as a highway—an endless journey into the Person of God. All of us walking in the light of relationship with God are at some point in that journey. As we "seek the Lord" and "search the Scriptures," we advance. The **A**ccelerated **C**hristian **T**raining **S**eries has been created to help us move on in that journey into the Lord regardless of whether we are new believers or seasoned saints of God. There is always more truth for us regardless of our place along the road. "His ways [are] past finding out" (Rom. 11:33b).

It is important that every believer follow a course such as this. Although the believer may be exposed to a variety of good biblical preaching, there must be a systematic seeking after truth to provide a foundation upon which to grow in relationship with the Person of Jesus. Imagine agreeing to marry someone of whom you had only seen a pencil sketching. It is our intention in this course of seeking to paint a full and vital portrait of the Christ who is alive in you.

If you are a new traveler on the highway of truth, you have begun the most exciting journey of your life. Many parallels can be drawn between the new believer and a newborn child. It would be a criminal act to leave an infant out in the cold or in a house without someone to give him attention and care. It is likewise a tragedy when the Church does not nurture newborn Christians. If newborns are going to be healthy and grow to

Introduction

maturity, they must be carefully and loving fed with the truth of the Word.

Truth Brings Maturity

The Christian life is a "growing up into Him in all things...until we come to the measure of the stature of the fullness of Christ" (see Eph. 4:13-15). It is important that we place ourselves under pastoral care if we are to "grow up." Even Jesus, who astonished the doctors and lawyers of His time, was entrusted to His parents' care. The Bible says, "Obey thse who rule over you, and be submissive: for they watch out for your souls" (Heb. 13:17). To reject the care of pastoral oversight is to reject God's plan to bring us to Himself and to leave ourselves open to error and the exit from the highway of our journey into the truth.

The ministry that God has given to the Church is five-phased with a threefold purpose. Ephesians 4:11 tells us that God has placed in the church apostles, prophets, evangelists, pastors and teachers. Their purpose is to mature, feed and motivate believers in their own calling and ministry. Only when this equipping is established in the life of the believer will they progress from spiritual newborn to spiritual childhood and on to spiritual adulthood.

In the life of every Christian there must come a point where we "put away childish things" (1 Cor. 13:11). As we become "rooted and grounded" in the basic principles of faith we are "no more children, tossed to and fro, and carried about with every wind of doctrine" (Eph. 4:14). As we grow and mature in the faith we are able to rise above our own problems and trials and reach out with power and confidence to minister the truth to the needs of those around us.

The Nature of God

How the Accelerated Christian Training Series Works

The **A**ccelerated **C**hristian **T**raining **S**eries has been designed to meet the crucial need for intensive training in the basic doctrines of the Christian faith. These doctrines are revealed in the context of relationship between God and man. It is designed as a self-instruction course in which believers can journey at their own pace. You will find review questions at the end of each section of material you have studied that will help you to retain what you've learned.

There is an exercise called "Dig a Little Deeper; Grow a Little Closer" at the end of each major section. These reflective questions are designed to help you synthesize the truths you have been taught and then apply them in a personal way. You will be invited to journal throughout the study of this book to provide you with a record of your new understanding and growth in God. Journaling will help you to grow in your ability to hear God's voice and adjust your life and understanding to His purpose.

Following this **A.C.T.S.** course will stimulate and accelerate your spiritual understanding and bring you to a more intimate knowledge of the Truth, who is Jesus Christ. We pray that you will grow in the awareness of the Lord's presence as He guides you to Himself through the study of His Word.

Two Companions for the Road

During this time of new growth in your spiritual life there will be questions that come to mind. You will meet two companions throughout this series on the road to truth. They are Newly Newborn and Truly Taughtright. Newly will ask some of the same questions that you ask, and Truly, his mentor, will give the answers.

I. The Nature of God

A. Who Is God?

God is the Creator and sustainer of all things.

Therefore know this day, and consider it in your heart, that the Lord Himself is God in heaven above and on the earth beneath; there is no other (Deuteronomy 4:39).

Thus says the Lord, the King of Israel, and his Redeemer, the Lord of hosts: "I am the First and I am the Last; besides Me there is no God" (Isaiah 44:6).

You alone are the Lord; You have made heaven, the heaven of heavens, with all their host, the earth and everything on it, the seas and all that is in them, and You preserve them all. The host of heaven worships You (Nehemiah 9:6).

B. How Is It Possible for Man to Know God?

1. We can know God because He dwells in His own creation.

The God who produced and formed the world and all the things in it, being Lord of Heaven and earth, does not dwell in handmade shrines. Neither is He served by human hands, as though He lacked anything, for it is He Himself who gives life and breath and all things to all people. So that they should seek God, in the hope that they may feel after Him and find Him, although He is not far from each one of us. For in Him we live and move and have our being; as even some of your own poets have said, For we are His offspring (Acts 17:24-25,27-28 AMP).

2. God's desire is to fellowship with all men as He did at first with Adam.

And they heard the sound of the Lord God walking in the garden in the cool of the day (Genesis 3:8a).

I will walk among you and be your God, and you shall be My people (Leviticus 26:12).

3. God can be seen in what He has created. God spoke all the laws of nature into existence at the very beginning.

The heavens declare the glory of God; and the firmament shows His handiwork (Psalm 19:1).

For since the creation of the world His invisible attributes are clearly seen, being understood by the things that are made, even His eternal power and Godhead, so that they are without excuse (Romans 1:20).

4. God has given us His Holy Scriptures, the Bible, to come to know Him.

You search the Scriptures, for in them you think you have eternal life; and these are they which testify of Me (John 5:39).

So then faith comes by hearing, and hearing by the word of God (Romans 10:17).

...From childhood you have known the Holy Scriptures, which are able to make you wise for

The Nature of God

salvation through faith which is in Christ Jesus (2 Timothy 3:15).

Let's Review What We Have Learned About God So Far.

1. God is the _____ and _____ of all things.

2. *Therefore know this day, and consider it in your heart, that the Lord Himself is God in _____ above and on the _____ beneath; there is no other* (Deuteronomy 4:39).

3. God has made provision to _____ in His own creation.

4. God can be _____ in what He has created.

5. It is God's desire to _____ with all men as He did at first with _____.

6. *So then _____ comes by hearing, and hearing by the _____ of God* (Romans 10:17).

C. What Is God?

God is a Spirit; He is without flesh and blood and is invisible to us.

Take careful heed to yourselves, for you saw no form when the Lord spoke to you at Horeb out of the midst of the fire, lest you act corruptly and make for yourselves a carved image in the form of any figure: the likeness of male or female, the likeness of any animal that is on the earth or the likeness of any winged bird that flies in the air, the likeness of anything that creeps on the ground or the likeness of any fish that is in the water beneath the earth. And take heed, lest you lift your eyes to heaven, and when you see the sun, the moon, and the stars, all the host of heaven, you feel driven to worship them and serve them, which the Lord your God has given to all the peoples under the whole heaven as a heritage (Deuteronomy 4:15-19).

God is Spirit, and those who worship Him must worship in spirit and truth (John 4:24).

Now to the King eternal, immortal, invisible, to God who alone is wise, be honor and glory forever and ever. Amen (1 Timothy 1:17).

D. What Qualities Might We Use to Describe God?

    1. God is omnipotent; He is all-powerful, able to do anything.

When Abram was ninety-nine years old, the Lord appeared to Abram and said to him, "I am Almighty God; walk before Me and be blameless" (Genesis 17:1).

But Jesus looked at them and said to them, "With men this is impossible, but with God all things are possible" (Matthew 19:26).

I know that You can do everything, and that no purpose of Yours can be withheld from You (Job 42:2).

The Nature of God

2.   God is omniscient; He is all-knowing. He knows all about me, what I think and where I am going.

O Lord, You have searched me and known me. You know my sitting down and my rising up; You understand my thought afar off. You comprehend my path and my lying down, and are acquainted with all my ways. For there is not a word on my tongue, but behold, O Lord, You know it altogether (Psalm 139:1-4).

...God is greater than our heart, and knows all things (1 John 3:20).

3.   God is omnipresent; He is present in all places and times at once.

"Can anyone hide himself in secret places, so I shall not see him?" says the Lord; "Do I not fill heaven and earth?" says the Lord (Jeremiah 23:24).

Where can I go from Your Spirit? Or where can I flee from Your presence? (Psalm 139:7)

4.   God is eternal; He lives outside of time and space.

Lord, You have been our dwelling place in all generations. Before the mountains were brought forth, or ever You had formed the earth and the world, even from everlasting to everlasting, You are God (Psalm 90:1-2).

But You, O Lord, shall endure forever, and the remembrance of Your name to all generations (Psalm 102:12).

The Nature of God

5. God never changes.

And God said unto Moses, I AM THAT I AM (Exodus 3:14a KJV).

For I am the Lord, I change not; therefore ye sons of Jacob are not consumed (Malachi 3:6 KJV).

Like a cloak You will fold them up, and they will be changed. But You are the same, and Your years will not fail (Hebrews 1:12).

Every good gift and every perfect gift is from above, and comes down from the Father of lights, with whom there is no variation or shadow of turning (James 1:17).

6. God is holy; He is utterly pure, without sin, without darkness.

But as He who called you is holy, you also be holy in all your conduct, because it is written, "Be holy, for I am holy" (1 Peter 1:15-16).

This is the message which we have heard from Him and declare to you, that God is light and in Him is no darkness at all (1 John 1:5).

And everyone who has this hope in Him purifies himself, just as He is pure…And you know that He was manifested to take away our sins, and in Him there is no sin (1 John 3:3,5).

Who shall not fear You, O Lord, and glorify Your name? For You alone are holy. For all nations shall come and worship before You, for Your judgments have been manifested (Revelation 15:4).

The Nature of God

7. God is just and fair to all people.

Far be it from You to do such a thing as this, to slay the righteous with the wicked, so that the righteous should be as the wicked; far be it from You! Shall not the Judge of all the earth do right? (Genesis 18:25)

He is the Rock, His work is perfect: for all His ways are judgment: a God of truth and without iniquity, just and right is He (Deuteronomy 32:4 KJV).

For the Lord your God is God of gods and Lord of lords, the great God, mighty and awesome, who shows no partiality nor takes a bribe. He administers justice for the fatherless and the widow, and loves the stranger, giving him food and clothing (Deuteronomy 10:17-18).

...He is coming, for He is coming to judge the earth. He shall judge the world with righteousness, and the peoples with His truth (Psalm 96:13).

But if our unrighteousness demonstrates the righteousness of God, what shall we say? Is God unjust who inflicts wrath? (I speak as a man.)...to demonstrate at the present time His righteousness, that He might be just and the justifier of the one who has faith in Jesus (Romans 3:5,26).

8. God is faithful; He will always do what He says He will do.

Be strong and of good courage, do not fear nor be afraid of them; for the Lord your God, He is the

The Nature of God

One who goes with you. He will not leave you nor forsake you (Deuteronomy 31:6).

Not a word failed of any good thing which the Lord had spoken to the house of Israel. All came to pass (Joshua 21:45).

God is faithful, by whom you were called into the fellowship of His Son, Jesus Christ our Lord (1 Corinthians 1:9).

If we are faithless, He remains faithful; He cannot deny Himself (2 Timothy 2:13).

9. God is good; He wants only the very best for us.

The Lord your God will make you abound in all the work of your hand, in the fruit of your body, in the increase of your livestock, and in the produce of your land for good. For the Lord will again rejoice over you for good as He rejoiced over your fathers (Deuteronomy 30:9).

Or do you despise the riches of His goodness, forbearance, and longsuffering, not knowing that the goodness of God leads you to repentance? (Romans 2:4)

Oh, taste and see that the Lord is good; blessed is the man who trusts in Him! (Psalm 34:8)

Every good gift and every perfect gift is from above, and comes down from the Father of lights, with whom there is no variation or shadow of turning (James 1:17).

The Nature of God

10. God is full of mercy; He delivers us from the bondage of sin and death.

You in Your mercy have led forth the people whom You have redeemed; You have guided them in Your strength to Your holy habitation (Exodus 15:13).

I will be glad and rejoice in Your mercy, for You have considered my trouble; You have known my soul in adversities, and have not shut me up into the hand of the enemy; You have set my feet in a wide place (Psalm 31:7-8).

For You, Lord, are good, and ready to forgive, and abundant in mercy to all those who call upon You (Psalm 86:5).

For I will be merciful to their unrighteousness, and their sins and their lawless deeds I will remember no more (Hebrews 8:12).

11. God is gracious; He shows us undeserved kindness; He does for us what we cannot do for ourselves.

For if you return to the Lord, your brethren and your children will be treated with compassion by those who lead them captive, so that they may come back to this land; for the Lord your God is gracious and merciful, and will not turn His face from you if you return to Him (2 Chronicles 30:9).

Let us therefore come boldly to the throne of grace, that we may obtain mercy and find grace to help in time of need (Hebrews 4:16).

The Nature of God

Even when we were dead in trespasses, made us alive together with Christ (by grace you have been saved) (Ephesians 2:5).

12. God is infinite; He is beyond measure and bigger than anything we can see.

Who has measured the waters in the hollow of His hand, measured heaven with a span and calculated the dust of the earth in a measure? Weighed the mountains in scales and the hills in a balance?...Behold, the nations are as a drop in a bucket, and are counted as the small dust on the scales; look, He lifts up the isles as a very little thing (Isaiah 40:12,15).

13. God is love.

He who does not love does not know God, for God is love (1 John 4:8).

Finally, brethren, farewell. Become complete. Be of good comfort, be of one mind, live in peace; and the God of love and peace will be with you (2 Corinthians 13:11).

Let's Review What We Have Learned About Who God Is.

1. God is a Spirit; He is without _____ and blood and _____ to us.

2. *Now to the King eternal, _____, invisible, to _____ who alone is wise, be honor and _____ forever and ever. Amen* (1 Timothy 1:17).

The Nature of God

3. List some of the words we use to describe God. For example: "God is omnipotent."

    a. God is _____

    b. God is _____

    c. God is _____

    d. God is _____

    e. God is _____

6. In God's mercy He _____ us from the bondage of sin and _____.

7. God is _____, utterly pure, without sin, without _____.

E. What Does the Term *Triune Godhead* Mean?

    1. God has revealed Himself in three manifestations (some people use the term *persons*)—Father, Son, and Holy Spirit. He is Father in creation, Son in redemption, and Holy Spirit in regeneration.

Hear, O Israel: The Lord our God, the Lord is One! (Deuteronomy 6:4)

And one cried to another and said: "Holy, holy, holy is the Lord of hosts; the whole earth is full of His glory!" (Isaiah 6:3)

"Go therefore and make disciples of all the nations, baptizing them in the name of the Father and of the Son and of the Holy Spirit" (Matthew 28:19).

The Nature of God

There is one body and one Spirit, just as you were called in one hope of your calling; one Lord, one faith, one baptism; one God and Father of all, who is above all, and through all, and in you all (Ephesians 4:3-6).

And without controversy great is the mystery of godliness: God was manifested in the flesh, justified in the Spirit, seen by angels, preached among the Gentiles, believed on in the world, received up in glory (1 Timothy 3:16).

For there are three that bear witness in heaven: the Father, the Word, and the Holy Spirit; and these three are one (1 John 5:7).

2. When we reach Heaven we will see only one God manifested as Father, Son, and Holy Spirit. A man can be father, a son, and a husband all at the same time but still only one man.

The Nature of God

F.   What Is God's Name?

1. There are many names for God throughout the Bible that tell us something about God, but God's name for Himself is *Yahweh* or *Yah*. This word could be translated "I AM." The English version of *Yahweh* is Jehovah. In His name God has revealed Himself as the "Great I AM."

And God said to Moses, "I AM WHO I AM." And He said, "Thus you shall say to the children of Israel, 'I AM has sent me to you'" (Exodus 3:14).

Sing to God, sing praises to His name; extol Him who rides on the clouds, by His name Yah, and rejoice before Him (Psalm 68:4).

2. God's name for Himself was holy and never pronounced by the people of Israel. Instead they substituted the word *LORD*. Wherever we see the word *LORD* in our Bibles, the original Hebrew word was the name *Yahweh*.

And whoever blasphemes the name of the Lord shall surely be put to death. All the congregation shall certainly stone him, the stranger as well as him who is born in the land. When he blasphemes the name of the Lord, he shall be put to death (Leviticus 24:16).

You shall not take the name of the Lord your God in vain, for the Lord will not hold him guiltless who takes His name in vain (Exodus 20:7).

3. Jesus also refers to Himself as "I AM," the same as the Father.

And He said to them, "You are from beneath; I am from above. You are of this world; I am not of this world. Therefore I said to you that you will die in your sins; for if you do not believe that I am He, you will die in your sins" (John 8:23-24).

I am the bread of life (John 6:48).

Then Jesus spoke to them again, saying, "I am the light of the world. He who follows Me shall not walk in darkness, but have the light of life" (John 8:12).

I am the good shepherd. The good shepherd gives His life for the sheep (John 10:11).

I am with you always, even to the end of the age (Matthew 28:20b).

G. **What Is the Difference Between the Lord of the Old Testament and the Lord of the New Testament?**

1. They are the same. The Lord of the Old Testament came in the flesh in the New Testament in the Person of the Lord Jesus Christ.

And the Word became flesh and dwelt among us, and we beheld His glory, the glory as of the only begotten of the Father, full of grace and truth (John 1:14).

Behold, the virgin shall be with child, and bear a Son, and they shall call His name Immanuel, which is translated, "God with us" (Matthew 1:23).

I and My Father are one (John 10:30).

The Nature of God

2. The Lord speaks of Himself using the same terms in both the Old and the New Testaments.

Thus says the Lord, the King of Israel, and his Redeemer, the Lord of hosts: "I am the First and I am the Last; besides Me there is no God" (Isaiah 44:6).

And when I saw Him, I fell at His feet as dead. But He laid His right hand on me, saying to me, "Do not be afraid; I am the First and the Last" (Revelation 1:17).

3. *Jesus* is the New Testament name for God. The name *Jesus* means, "Jehovah has become salvation." Jesus commissioned the disciples to baptize in the name of the Father, the Son, and the Holy Spirit. The apostles obeyed this commission by baptizing in the name of Jesus Christ.

The Nature of God

Then Peter said to them, "Repent, and let every one of you be baptized in the name of Jesus Christ for the remission of sins; and you shall receive the gift of the Holy Spirit" (Acts 2:38).

H. Who Is the Holy Spirit and How Is He Related to Jesus Christ?

1. Jesus is identified with the Holy Spirit because of the Spirit's activity in His life and ministry. The Holy Spirit is the anointing of God. The Greek word for anointing is the same word from which we get the word *Christ*.

"The Spirit of the Lord is upon Me, because He has anointed Me to preach the gospel to the poor; He has sent Me to heal the brokenhearted, to proclaim liberty to the captives and recovery of sight to the blind, to set at liberty those who are oppressed; to proclaim the acceptable year of the Lord"...And He began to say to them, "Today this Scripture is fulfilled in your hearing" (Luke 4:18-19,21).

And Simon Peter answered and said, Thou art the Christ, the Son of the Living God (Matthew 16:16 KJV).

2. The same Holy Spirit who was active in the life and ministry of Jesus Christ was released into His Body on earth, the Church, when He ascended to heaven. "I will not leave you orphans; I will come to you" (John 14:18).

But when the Helper comes, whom I shall send to you from the Father, the Spirit of truth who proceeds from the Father, He will testify of Me (John 15:26).

The Nature of God

3. The Holy Spirit and the Spirit of Christ are the same Person, dwelling in His Body, the Church.

But you are not in the flesh but in the Spirit, if indeed the Spirit of God dwells in you. Now if anyone does not have the Spirit of Christ, he is not His. And if Christ is in you, the body is dead because of sin, but the Spirit is life because of righteousness. But if the Spirit of Him who raised Jesus from the dead dwells in you, He who raised Christ from the dead will also give life to your mortal bodies through His Spirit who dwells in you (Romans 8:9-11).

Let's Review What We Have Learned About Who God Is.

1. The word _____ is not found in the Bible. However, God has revealed Himself in three manifestations—

The Nature of God

_____ , _____ , and _____ _____ .

2. *For there are* _____ *that bear witness in heaven: the* _____, *the* _____, *and the Holy Spirit; and these three are* _____ (1 John 5:7).

3. *Hear, O Israel, the Lord our God, the Lord is* _____ (Deuteronomy 6:4).

4. Wherever we see the word _____ in our Bibles, the original Hebrew word was the name *Yahweh*.

5. *If you do not believe that* _____ *He, you will die in your sins* (John 8:24b).

6. *I am the* _____ *of life* (John 6:48).

7. The Lord of the Old Testament came in the New Testament in the Person of _____ .

8. The Holy Spirit is the _____ manifestation of the Godhead.

9. The Greek word for anointing is the same word from which we get the word _____ .

Dig a Little Deeper; Grow a Little Closer

Read the following Bible passage and answer the questions below.

And the Lord passed before him and proclaimed, "The Lord, the Lord God, merciful and gracious, longsuffering, and abounding in goodness and truth, keeping mercy for thousands, forgiving iniquity and transgression and sin, by no means clearing the guilty, visiting

The Nature of God

the iniquity of the fathers upon the children and the children's children to the third and the fourth generation." So Moses made haste and bowed his head toward the earth, and worshiped (Exodus 34:6-8).

1. Read the preceding text and pick out the many words that God used to talk about Himself. List each word here and then what you hear the Lord telling you about Himself.

_____

_____

_____

_____

_____

2. Think back on your life and God's gracious calling into salvation in Christ Jesus. How have any or all of these words become real to you personally?

_____

_____

_____

_____

_____

3. Pray now, repeating those words back to God as your own personal song of praise.

The Nature of God

Review Notes

The Nature of God

The Nature of God

The Nature of God

The Nature of God

The Nature of God

The Nature of God

II. The Bible

A. **What Is the Bible?**

1. The Bible is the inspired or "God-breathed" word of God.

All Scripture is given by inspiration of God, and is profitable for doctrine, for reproof, for correction, for instruction in righteousness, that the man of God may be complete, thoroughly equipped for every good work (2 Timothy 3:16-17).

For this reason we also thank God without ceasing, because when you received the word of God which you heard from us, you welcomed it not as the word of men, but as it is in truth, the word of God, which also effectively works in you who believe (1 Thessalonians 2:13).

2. The Holy Spirit moved upon the holy men who wrote the Bible.

For prophecy never came by the will of man, but holy men of God spoke as they were moved by the Holy Spirit (2 Peter 1:21).

The Spirit of the Lord spoke by me, and His word was on my tongue (2 Samuel 23:2).

As He spoke by the mouth of His holy prophets, who have been since the world began (Luke 1:70).

3. Every word of the Bible is God's; therefore the Bible is without error.

Your word is truth (John 17:17b).

The Nature of God

Heaven and earth will pass away, but My words will by no means pass away (Matthew 24:35).

The Scripture cannot be broken (John 10:35b).

4. The Bible is given to us to give us wisdom that leads to salvation through faith in Christ Jesus.

And that from childhood you have known the Holy Scriptures, which are able to make you wise for salvation through faith which is in Christ Jesus (2 Timothy 3:15).

5. The Bible enables us to live a holy life.

That the man of God may be complete, thoroughly equipped for every good work (2 Timothy 3:17).

6. The Bible tells us about Jesus Christ.

You search the Scriptures, for in them you think you have eternal life; and these are they which testify of Me (John 5:39).

7. The Bible is the testimony of God that, when read, renews our minds. As we search the Scriptures diligently and reverently and listen while they are being read, they guide us in our daily living.

The law of the Lord is perfect, converting the soul; the testimony of the Lord is sure, making wise the simple (Psalm 19:7).

How can a young man cleanse his way? By taking heed according to Your word (Psalm 119:9).

The Bible

B. What Are the Results of Obeying the Bible?

1. As we obey the Bible we are blessed.

This Book of the Law shall not depart from your mouth, but you shall meditate in it day and night, that you may observe to do according to all that is written in it. For then you will make your way prosperous, and then you will have good success (Joshua 1:8).

Blessed are those who hear the word of God and keep it (Luke 11:28).

Your words were found, and I ate them, and Your word was to me the joy and rejoicing of my heart; for I am called by Your name, O Lord God of hosts (Jeremiah 15:16).

2. As we obey the Bible we display our love for Jesus.

Then Jesus said to those Jews who believed Him, "If you abide in My word, you are My disciples indeed. And you shall know the truth, and the truth shall make you free" (John 8:31-32).

Jesus answered and said to him, "If anyone loves Me, he will keep My word; and My Father will love him, and We will come to him and make Our home with him" (John 14:23).

3. As we obey the Bible we avoid sin.

But his delight is in the law of the Lord, and in His law he meditates day and night (Psalm 1:2).

Your word I have hidden in my heart, that I might not sin against You! (Psalm 119:11)

C. What Are the Two Great Divisions in the Bible?

1. The first part of the Bible is the Old Testament, which contains the Law. The Law is a guideline that teaches us how to live in harmony with God and man. It is the basis for all government.

Speak to all the congregation of the children of Israel, and say to them: "You shall be holy, for I the Lord your God am holy" (Leviticus 19:2).

You shall therefore keep His statutes and His commandments which I command you today, that it may go well with you and with your children after you, and that you may prolong your days in the land which the Lord your God is giving you for all time (Deuteronomy 4:40).

The Bible

And these words which I command you today shall be in your heart. You shall teach them diligently to your children, and shall talk of them when you sit in your house, when you walk by the way, when you lie down, and when you rise up (Deuteronomy 6:6-7).

2. The second part of the Bible is called the New Testament. It contains the Gospel, which is the good news of our salvation in Christ Jesus.

In this the love of God was manifested toward us, that God has sent His only begotten Son into the world, that we might live through Him (1 John 4:9).

Then the angel said to them, "Do not be afraid, for behold, I bring you good tidings of great joy which will be to all people. For there is born to you this day in the city of David a Savior, who is Christ the Lord" (Luke 2:10-11).

For God so loved the world that He gave His only begotten Son, that whoever believes in Him should not perish but have everlasting life (John 3:16).

Moreover, brethren, I declare to you the gospel which I preached to you, which also you received and in which you stand...For I delivered to you first of all that which I also received: that Christ died for our sins according to the Scriptures, and that He was buried, and that He rose again the third day according to the Scriptures (1 Corinthians 15:1,3-4).

The Nature of God

      3.   The difference between the Law and the Gospel is that the Law teaches what man can and cannot do, and the Gospel teaches what God has done and still does. The Law shows us our sin, but the Gospel shows us God's grace through Jesus Christ.

For what the law could not do in that it was weak through the flesh, God did by sending His own Son in the likeness of sinful flesh, on account of sin: He condemned sin in the flesh (Romans 8:3).

D.   **What Are the Books of the Bible?**

      1.   The Bible is not a single book but a collection of 66 books written under the inspiration of the Holy Spirit by 44 different writers. The books of the Bible were written over a period of 2000 years yet its books provide a perfect harmony of doctrines.

      2.   There are many different kinds of books in the Bible:

17 Old Testament Books of History

Genesis	Joshua	1 and 2 Chronicles
Exodus	Judges	Ezra
Leviticus	Ruth	Nehemiah
Numbers	1 and 2 Samuel	Esther
Deuteronomy	1 and 2 Kings	

5 Old Testament Books of Poetry

Job	Proverbs	Song of Solomon
Psalms	Ecclesiastes	

The Bible

17 Old Testament Prophetic Books

Major Prophets	**Minor Prophets**		
Isaiah Ezekiel	Hosea	Jonah	Zephaniah
Jeremiah Daniel	Joel	Micah	Haggai
Lamentations (also	Amos	Nahum	Zechariah
considered poetical)	Obadiah	Habakkuk	Malachi

5 New Testament Historical Books

Matthew	Luke	Acts
Mark	John	

21 Books of New Testament Doctrine

Romans	1 and 2 Thessalonians	James
1 and 2 Corinthians	1 and 2 Timothy	1 and 2 Peter
Galatians	Titus	1, 2, 3 John
Ephesians	Philemon	Jude
Philippians	Colossians	Hebrews

1 New Testament Prophetic Book

Revelation

E. What Are the Benefits of Studying the Bible?

1. Studying the Bible uncovers sin.

For the word of God is living and powerful, and sharper than any two-edged sword, piercing even to the division of soul and spirit, and of joints and marrow, and is a discerner of the thoughts and intents of the heart (Hebrews 4:12).

And Nehemiah, who was the governor, Ezra the priest and scribe, and the Levites who taught the people said to all the people, "This day is holy to the Lord your God; do not mourn nor weep." For all the people wept, when they heard the words of the Law (Nehemiah 8:9).

2. Studying the Bible cleanses us from the pollution of sin.

How can a young man cleanse his way? By taking heed according to Your word (Psalms 119:9).

The law of the Lord is perfect, converting the soul; the testimony of the Lord is sure, making wise the simple (Psalm 19:7).

You are already clean because of the word which I have spoken to you (John 15:3).

3. Studying the Bible gives us strength for our lives.

But He answered and said, "It is written, 'Man shall not live by bread alone, but by every word that proceeds from the mouth of God'" (Matthew 4:4).

The Bible

The fear of the Lord is clean...sweeter also than honey and the honeycomb (Psalm 19:9-10).

4. Studying the Bible gives us direction for our lives.

Therefore whoever hears these sayings of Mine, and does them, I will liken him to a wise man who built his house on the rock: and the rain descended, the floods came, and the winds blew and beat on that house; and it did not fall, for it was founded on the rock. But everyone who hears these sayings of Mine, and does not do them, will be like a foolish man who built his house on the sand: and the rain descended, the floods came, and the winds blew and beat on that house; and it fell. And great was its fall (Matthew 7:24-27).

Then the Lord answered me and said: "Write the vision and make it plain on tablets, that he may run who reads it" (Habakkuk 2:2).

5. Studying the Bible provides us a sword for victory over sin.

Your word I have hidden in my heart, that I might not sin against You! (Psalm 119:11)

And take the helmet of salvation, and the sword of the Spirit, which is the word of God (Ephesians 6:17).

I have written to you, fathers, because you have known Him who is from the beginning. I have written to you, young men, because you are strong, and the word of God abides in you, and you have overcome the wicked one (1 John 2:14).

And they overcame him by the blood of the Lamb and by the word of their testimony, and they did not love their lives to the death (Revelation 12:11).

6. Studying the Bible gives us power to pray.

If you abide in Me, and My words abide in you, you will ask what you desire, and it shall be done for you (John 15:7).

Delight yourself also in the Lord, and He shall give you the desires of your heart (Psalm 37:4).

F. How Often Should We Read From This Collection of Books?

We should read from the Bible every day.

Oh, how I love Your law! It is my meditation all the day (Psalm 119:97).

These were more fair-minded than those in Thessalonica, in that they received the word with all readiness, and searched the Scriptures daily to find out whether these things were so (Acts 17:11).

G. What Other Books Should Supplement My Study of the Bible?

1. A good Bible dictionary, which defines various words and subjects of the Bible

2. An exhaustive concordance, which shows us where certain words occur throughout the Bible

The Bible

3. A Bible handbook, which gives a general background and commentary on the passages we are reading

H. What Should We Do After Reading the Bible?

We should meditate on what we have read, then soak in its truths and allow them to become part of us.

Make me understand the way of Your precepts; so shall I meditate on Your wondrous works (Psalm 119:27).

But his delight is in the law of the Lord, and in His law he meditates day and night (Psalm 1:2).

Finally, brethren, whatever things are true, whatever things are noble, whatever things are just, whatever things are pure, whatever things are lovely, whatever things are of good report, if there is any virtue and if there is anything praiseworthy—meditate on these things (Philippians 4:8).

The Nature of God

Let's Review What We Have Learned About the Bible.

1. The Bible is the inspired or _____ word of God.

2. *For prophecy never came by the will of man, but _____ of God spoke as they were moved by the _____* (2 Peter 1:21).

3. Every word of the Bible is _____, therefore the Bible is without _____.

4. *You search the _____, for in them you think you have eternal life; and these are they which testify of _____* (John 5:39).

5. We are blessed as we _____ the Bible.

6. List three benefits of studying the Bible.

_____

_____

_____

7. The Bible is a _____ of _____ books written by 44 different writers under the _____ of the Holy Spirit.

8. We should read the Bible _____.

9. *But his delight is in the law of the Lord, and in His law he _____ day and night* (Psalm 1:2).

10. The Bible is written in two great divisions: The _____ Testament and the _____ Testament.

The Bible

Dig a Little Deeper; Grow a Little Closer

Read the following Bible passage and answer the questions below.

All Scripture is given by inspiration of God, and is profitable for doctrine, for reproof, for correction, for instruction in righteousness, that the man of God may be complete, thoroughly equipped for every good work (2 Timothy 3:16-17).

1. What four things does this passage tell us that the Bible is profitable for?

_____

_____

_____

_____

2. Now express in your own words what those four things mean. Perhaps it would be helpful to look them up in a dictionary.

_____

_____

_____

_____

3. What two words in verse 17 describe the result of our study of the Word of God?

_____

_____

The Nature of God

Review Notes

The Bible

The Nature of God

The Bible

The Nature of God

The Bible

The Nature of God

III. The Creation

A. What Did God Create?

God created all that is seen and unseen; everything that is in heaven and earth; the spirit realm and the natural realm.

In the beginning God created the heavens and the earth (Genesis 1:1).

For by Him all things were created that are in heaven and that are on earth, visible and invisible, whether thrones or dominions or principalities or powers. All things were created through Him and for Him. And He is before all things, and in Him all things consist (Colossians 1:16-17).

By faith we understand that the worlds were framed by the word of God, so that the things which are seen were not made of things which are visible (Hebrews 11:3).

B. What Did God Create First?

God created the heavens, the unseen realm of angels or ministering spirits.

Where were you when I laid the foundations of the earth? Tell Me, if you have understanding...when the morning stars sang together, and all the sons of God shouted for joy? (Job 38:4,7)

C. What Are Angels?

1. Angels are invisible ministering spirits created by God to do His will.

The Nature of God

Bless the Lord, you His angels, who excel in strength, who do His word, heeding the voice of His word. Bless the Lord, all you His hosts, you ministers of His, who do His pleasure (Psalm 103:20-21).

Who makes His angels spirits, His ministers a flame of fire (Psalm 104:4).

Are they not all ministering spirits sent forth to minister for those who will inherit salvation? (Hebrews 1:14)

2.   There are good angels and evil angels.

His tail drew a third of the stars of heaven and threw them to the earth. And the dragon stood before the woman who was ready to give birth, to devour her Child as soon as it was born...And war broke out in heaven: Michael and his angels fought with the dragon; and the dragon and his angels fought...So the great dragon was cast out,

The Creation

that serpent of old, called the devil and satan, who deceives the whole world; he was cast to the earth, and his angels were cast out with him (Revelation 12:4,7,9).

D. What Does the Bible Tell Us About Good Angels?

1. Good angels are greater in number and power than evil angels.

The chariots of God are twenty thousand, even thousands of thousands; the Lord is among them as in Sinai, in the Holy Place (Psalm 68:17).

And suddenly there was with the angel a multitude of the heavenly host praising God and saying (Luke 2:13).

...angels, who are greater in power and might (2 Peter 2:11a).

2. Good angels praise God.

You alone are the Lord; You have made heaven, the heaven of heavens, with all their host, the earth and everything on it, the seas and all that is in them, and You preserve them all. The host of heaven worships You (Nehemiah 9:6).

In the year that King Uzziah died, I saw the Lord sitting on a throne, high and lifted up, and the train of His robe filled the temple. Above it stood seraphim; each one had six wings: with two he covered his face, with two he covered his feet, and with two he flew. And one cried to another and said:

"Holy, holy, holy is the Lord of hosts; the whole earth is full of His glory!" (Isaiah 6:1-3)

Then the Spirit lifted me up, and I heard behind me a great thunderous voice: "Blessed is the glory of the Lord from His place!" I also heard the noise of the wings of the living creatures that touched one another, and the noise of the wheels beside them, and a great thunderous noise (Ezekiel 3:12-13).

3. Good angels carry out God's commands and serve God's purpose, especially among children.

Are they not all ministering spirits sent forth to minister for those who will inherit salvation? (Hebrews 1:14)

The angel of the Lord encamps all around those who fear Him, and delivers them (Psalm 34:7).

For He shall give His angels charge over you, to keep you in all your ways (Psalm 91:11).

Now behold, an angel of the Lord stood by him, and a light shone in the prison; and he struck Peter on the side and raised him up, saying, "Arise quickly!" And his chains fell off his hands (Acts 12:7).

Take heed that you do not despise one of these little ones, for I say to you that in heaven their angels always see the face of My Father who is in heaven (Matthew 18:10).

The Creation

E. **What Does the Bible Tell Us About Evil Angels?**

    1. Evil angels were created to be holy but rebelled against God and are now separated from Him forever.

How you are fallen from heaven, O lucifer, son of the morning! How you are cut down to the ground, you who weakened the nations! (Isaiah 14:12)

Then He will also say to those on the left hand, "Depart from Me, you cursed, into the everlasting fire prepared for the devil and his angels" (Matthew 25:41).

For if God did not spare the angels who sinned, but cast them down to hell and delivered them into chains of darkness, to be reserved for judgment (2 Peter 2:4).

    2. Evil angels are cunning, powerful, and great in number.

For we do not wrestle against flesh and blood, but against principalities, against powers, against the rulers of the darkness of this age, against spiritual hosts of wickedness in the heavenly places (Ephesians 6:12).

Then He asked him, "What is your name?" And he answered, saying, "My name is legion; for we are many" (Mark 5:9).

    3. Evil angels are the enemies of God and also of man. They endeavor to destroy the works of God.

The Nature of God

You are of your father the devil, and the desires of your father you want to do. He was a murderer from the beginning, and does not stand in the truth, because there is no truth in him. When he speaks a lie, he speaks from his own resources, for he is a liar and the father of it (John 8:44).

Be sober, be vigilant; because your adversary the devil walks about like a roaring lion, seeking whom he may devour. Resist him, steadfast in the faith, knowing that the same sufferings are experienced by your brotherhood in the world (1 Peter 5:8-9).

F.   Are Angels to Be Worshiped?

1.   No. We are forbidden to worship angels.

Let no one cheat you of your reward, taking delight in false humility and worship of angels, intruding into those things which he has not seen, vainly puffed up by his fleshly mind (Colossians 2:18).

The Creation

Who exchanged the truth of God for the lie, and worshiped and served the creature rather than the Creator, who is blessed forever. Amen (Romans 1:25).

And I fell at his feet to worship him. But he said to me, "See that you do not do that! I am your fellow servant, and of your brethren who have the testimony of Jesus. Worship God! For the testimony of Jesus is the spirit of prophecy" (Revelation 19:10).

2. It is dangerous to become angel conscious. Even an angel can lead us astray.

But even if we, or an angel from heaven, preach any other gospel to you than what we have preached to you, let him be accursed (Galatians 1:8).

G. Who Is Lucifer?

1. Lucifer was the chief angel of heaven. He was also called the "son of the morning." He was an anointed cherub of God covering the throne of God. But he rebelled against God and was cast out of heaven.

How you are fallen from heaven, O lucifer, son of the morning! How you are cut down to the ground, you who weakened the nations! For you have said in your heart: "I will ascend into heaven, I will exalt my throne above the stars of God; I will also sit on the mount of the congregation on the farthest sides of the north; I will ascend above the heights of the clouds, I will be like the Most High." Yet you

The Nature of God

shall be brought down to Sheol, to the lowest depths of the Pit (Isaiah 14:12-15).

2. Lucifer was created beautiful. His appearance was as precious stones and his voice sounded like a great pipe organ. He was perfect in beauty and wisdom.

Thus says the Lord God: "You were the seal of perfection, full of wisdom and perfect in beauty. You were in Eden, the garden of God; every precious stone was your covering: the sardius, topaz, and diamond, beryl, onyx, and jasper, sapphire, turquoise, and emerald with gold. The workmanship of your timbrels and pipes was prepared for you on the day you were created. You were the anointed cherub who covers; I established you; you were on the holy mountain of God; you walked back and forth in the midst of fiery stones. You were perfect in your ways from the day you were created, till iniquity was found in you. By the abundance of your trading you became filled with violence within, and you sinned; therefore I cast you as a profane thing out of the mountain of God; and I destroyed you, O covering cherub, from the midst of the fiery stones" (Ezekiel 28:12b-16).

3. Lucifer became the devil, satan, and those that followed him became demons.

Your heart was lifted up because of your beauty; you corrupted your wisdom for the sake of your splendor; I cast you to the ground, I laid you before kings, that they might gaze at you (Ezekiel 28:17).

The Creation

4. Lucifer and his demons are forever fallen from heaven. Some are held in everlasting chains and others roam the earth as enemies of God and man.

And the Lord said to satan, "From where do you come?" So satan answered the Lord and said, "From going to and fro on the earth, and from walking back and forth on it" (Job 1:7).

And He said to them, "I saw satan fall like lightning from heaven" (Luke 10:18).

Be sober, be vigilant; because your adversary the devil walks about like a roaring lion, seeking whom he may devour (1 Peter 5:8).

For if God did not spare the angels who sinned, but cast them down to hell and delivered them into chains of darkness, to be reserved for judgment (2 Peter 2:4).

The Nature of God

And the angels who did not keep their proper domain, but left their own abode, He has reserved in everlasting chains under darkness for the judgment of the great day (Jude 1:6).

H. What Is Hell?

Hell is the abode of the devil and his demons. Only those who refuse Christ go to hell because there is no other place for them to go.

The wicked shall be turned into hell, and all the nations that forget God (Psalm 9:17).

Then He will also say to those on the left hand, "Depart from Me, you cursed, into the everlasting fire prepared for the devil and his angels" (Matthew 25:41).

Then the fifth angel sounded: And I saw a star fallen from heaven to the earth. To him was given the key to the bottomless pit. And he opened the bottomless pit, and smoke arose out of the pit like the smoke of a great furnace. So the sun and the air were darkened because of the smoke of the pit (Revelation 9:1-2).

I. Who Has Power Over Satan and His Demons?

    1. God and the Church of Jesus Christ have power and authority over satan and all his demons.

And Jesus came and spoke to them, saying, "All authority has been given to Me in heaven and on earth" (Matthew 28:18).

The Creation

Behold, I give you the authority to trample on serpents and scorpions, and over all the power of the enemy, and nothing shall by any means hurt you (Luke 10:19).

Which He worked in Christ when He raised Him from the dead and seated Him at His right hand in the heavenly places, far above all principality and power and might and dominion, and every name that is named, not only in this age but also in that which is to come. And He put all things under His feet, and gave Him to be head over all things to the church, which is His body, the fullness of Him who fills all in all…and raised us up together, and made us sit together in the heavenly places in Christ Jesus (Ephesians 1:20-23; 2:6).

J.   What Did God Create After the Spirit Realm?

1. In six days God created the physical universe that we can see.

By faith we understand that the worlds were framed by the word of God, so that the things which are seen were not made of things which are visible (Hebrews 11:3).

By the word of the Lord the heavens were made, and all the host of them by the breath of His mouth (Psalm 33:6).

You are worthy, O Lord, to receive glory and honor and power; for You created all things, and by Your will they exist and were created (Revelation 4:11).

The Nature of God

2. God formed all living creatures on the earth.

Then God said, "Let the earth bring forth the living creature according to its kind: cattle and creeping thing and beast of the earth, each according to its kind"; and it was so (Genesis 1:24).

I have made the earth, the man and the beast that are on the ground, by My great power and by My outstretched arm, and have given it to whom it seemed proper to Me (Jeremiah 27:5).

3. God created man in His own image and gave him dominion over all of the earth. Man was unique in that God breathed His own breath of life into him and made him spiritually alive.

Then God said, "Let Us make man in Our image, according to Our likeness; let them have dominion over the fish of the sea, over the birds of the air, and over the cattle, over all the earth and over every creeping thing that creeps on the earth." So God created man in His own image; in the image of God He created him; male and female He created them (Genesis 1:26-27).

And the Lord God formed man of the dust of the ground, and breathed into his nostrils the breath of life; and man became a living being (Genesis 2:7).

4. God created man as a special creation, not as the product of evolution. God made man

The Creation

alive with His very breath so that man would seek after God.

The Spirit of God has made me, and the breath of the Almighty gives me life (Job 33:4).

Know that the Lord, He is God; it is He who has made us, and not we ourselves; we are His people and the sheep of His pasture (Psalm 100:3).

And He has made from one blood every nation of men to dwell on all the face of the earth, and has determined their preappointed times and the boundaries of their dwellings, so that they should seek the Lord, in the hope that they might grope for Him and find Him, though He is not far from each one of us (Acts 17:26-27).

Let's Review What We Have Learned About Creation.

1. Angels are invisible _____ spirits created by God to do His _____.

2. Good angels are greater in _____ and _____ than evil angels.

3. Evil angels are the enemies of _____ and also _____.

4. *For He shall give His _____ charge over you, to _____ you in all your ways* (Psalm 91:11).

5. Lucifer became the _____, satan, and those that followed him became _____.

The Nature of God

6. God and the _____ of Jesus Christ have been given _____ and _____ over satan and all his demons.

7. *In the beginning God created the _____ and the _____* (Genesis 1:1).

8. God created man in His own _____ and gave him _____ over all of the earth.

9. Man was unique in that God _____ His own breath of life into him and made him _____ alive.

10. Man was a special _____ of God, not the product of _____.

Dig a Little Deeper; Grow a Little Closer

Read the following passage of Scripture.

When I consider Your heavens, the work of Your fingers, the moon and the stars, which You have ordained, what is man that You are mindful of him, and the son of man that You visit him? For You have made him a little lower than the angels, and You have crowned him with glory and honor. You have made him to have dominion over the works of Your hands; you have put all things under his feet, all sheep and oxen—even the beasts of the field, the birds of the air, and the fish of the sea that pass through the paths of the seas. O Lord, our Lord, how excellent is Your name in all the earth! (Psalm 8:3-9)

1. As you read these verses that speak of God's creation, notice and write down what they say about man. (You!)

The Creation

_____
_____
_____
_____
_____
_____

2.   Are there areas in your life that are not "under your feet"? Write them down and then compare them to the truths you have learned from this section of teaching on creation. Write down here what the Lord is speaking to you regarding your position in those areas of struggle.

_____
_____
_____
_____
_____
_____
_____

Taking Possession of the Truth:

We encourage you to journal here what the Lord has spoken to you during your study in this first of seven sections on the nature of God, the Bible, and creation. As you journal what the Lord has spoken to you, you will take possession of the truth.

The Nature of God

Review Notes

The Creation

The Nature of God

The Creation

The Nature of God

The Creation

The Nature of God

The Creation

Be sure to enter into the journal in this book how God responds to what you have prayed.

Books in the *Laying the FOUNDATION* Series:

Book 1—The Nature of God
- I. The Nature of God
- II. The Bible
- III. The Creation

Book 2—The Nature of Man
- I. The Nature of Man
- II. The Fall of Man
- III. The Seed of Rebellion Continues

Book 3—A Call to Faith and Obedience
- I. Abraham: The Father of Faith and Obedience
- II. Israel: Called to Be the People of God

Book 4—From Covenant to Kingdom
- I. Taking Possession of the Promises of God
- II. Establishing the Kingdom
- III. The Message of the Prophets
- IV. Restoring the Remnant of Israel

Book 5—The New Covenant
- I. The New Covenant
- II. The Person of Jesus Christ
- III. The Nature of Jesus Christ
- IV. The Humiliation of Jesus Christ

Book 6—Jesus Christ, Servant of God
- I. Wounded for Our Transgressions
- II. Bruised for Our Iniquities
- III. Chastised for Our Peace
- IV. Scourged for Our Healing

Book 7—The Exaltation of Christ
- I. The Exaltation of Jesus Christ
- II. Jesus and the Kingdom of God

Summary

More Titles by Dr. Mark Hanby

➤ YOU HAVE NOT MANY FATHERS

"My son, give me your heart." So says the proverb, echoing the heart and passion of our Father in heaven. God has spiritual "dads" all over the world whom He has filled with wisdom, knowledge, compassion, and most of all, love for those young in the faith. You do not have to go through your life untrained and unloved; uncared for and forgotten. There are fathers in Christ who are waiting to pour all they have into your heart, as Elijah did for Elisha. "My son, give me your heart."
ISBN 1-56043-166-0

➤ YOU HAVE NOT MANY FATHERS STUDY GUIDE
ISBN 0-7684-2036-9

➤ THE HOUSE THAT GOD BUILT

Beyond whatever man can desire is a God-given pattern for the life of the Church. Here Dr. Hanby unfolds practical applications from the design of the Tabernacle that allow us to become the house God is building today.
ISBN 1-56043-091-5

➤ THE HOUSE THAT GOD BUILT STUDY GUIDE
ISBN 0-7684-2048-2

➤ THE RENEWING OF THE HOLY GHOST

Do you need renewal? Everything in the natural, from birds to blood cells, must either undergo a process of renewal or enter into death. Our spiritual life is no different. With this book, your renewal can begin today!
ISBN 1-56043-031-1

➤ ANOINTING THE UNSANCTIFIED

The anointing is more than a talented performance or an emotional response. In this book, Dr. Hanby details the essential ingredients of directional relationship that allow the Spirit of God to flow down upon the Body of Christ—and from us to the needs of a dying world.
ISBN 1-56043-071-0

➤ PERCEIVING THE WHEEL OF GOD

On the potter's wheel, a lump of clay yields to a necessary process of careful pressure and constant twisting. Similarly, the form of true faith is shaped by a trusting response to God in a suffering situation. This book offers essential understanding for victory through the struggles of life.
ISBN 1-56043-109-1

Available at your local Christian bookstore.

For more information and sample chapters, visit www.destinyimage.com